The

Poems

of

Abraham Lincoln

ABRAHAM LINCOLN
1809-1865

The

Poems

of

Abraham Lincoln

Applewood Books

Bedford, Massachusetts

The Poems of
Abraham Lincoln

Abraham Lincoln was America's sixteenth
President. His career as a statesman is well-
known. Little known is that he was a great
lover of poetry. His speeches and writings
are filled with great and beautiful prose,
but he only wrote three poems.

In 1844, while campaigning for Henry
Clay, Lincoln returned to Indiana, where
he was raised and his mother and sister
were buried. There, after being gone
fifteen years, the place and the people
aroused memories of his childhood that
prompted him to write the poems.

My Childhood's Home

My childhood's home I see again,
     And sadden with the view;
And still, as memory crowds my brain,
     There's pleasure in it too.

O Memory! thou midway world
     'Twixt earth and paradise,
Where things decayed and loved ones lost
     In dreamy shadows rise,

And, freed from all that's earthly vile,
　　Seem hallowed, pure, and bright,
Like scenes in some enchanted isle
　　All bathed in liquid light.

As dusky mountains please the eye
　　When twilight chases day;
As bugle-notes that, passing by,
　　In distance die away;

As leaving some grand waterfall,
　　We, lingering, list its roar—
So memory will hallow all
　　We've known, but know no more.

Near twenty years have passed away
Since here I bid farewell
To woods and fields, and scenes of play,
And playmates loved so well.

Where many were, but few remain
Of old familiar things;
But seeing them, to mind again
The lost and absent brings.

The friends I left the parting day,
How changed, as time has sped!
Young childhood grown, strong manhood gray,
And half of all are dead.

I hear the loved survivors tell
      How nought from death could save
Till every sound appears a knell,
      And every spot a grave.

I range the fields with pensive tread
      And pace the hollow rooms,
And feel (companion of the dead)
      I'm living in the tombs.

But Here's an Object…

But here's an object more of dread
      Than aught the grave contains—
A human form with reason fled,
      While wretched life remains.

Poor Matthew! Once of genius bright,
      A fortune-favored child—
Now locked for aye, in mental night,
      A haggard mad-man wild.

Poor Matthew! I have ne'er forgot,
    When first, with maddened will,
Yourself you maimed, your father fought,
    And mother strove to kill;

When terror spread, and neighbors ran,
    Your dangerous strength to bind;
And soon, a howling crazy man,
    Your limbs were fast confined.

How then you strove and shrieked aloud,
    Your bones and sinews bared;
And fiendish on the gazing crowd,
    With burning eyeballs glared—

And begged and swore, and wept and prayed,
    With maniac laughter joined—
How fearful were those signs displayed
    By pangs that killed the mind!

And when at length, tho' drear and long
    Time soothed thy fiercer woes,
How plaintively thy mournful song
    Upon the still night rose!

I've heard it oft, as if I dreamed,
    Far distant, sweet and lone,
The funeral dirge, it ever seemed
    Of reason dead and gone.

To drink its strains I've stole away,
         All stealthily and still,
Ere yet the rising god of day
         Had streaked the eastern hill.

Air held his breath; trees, with the spell,
         Seemed sorrowing angels round,
Whose swelling tears in dewdrops fell
         Upon the listening ground.

But this is past, and naught remains
         That raised thee o'er the brute;
Thy piercing shrieks and soothing strains
         Are like, forever mute.

Now fare thee well—more thou the cause
  Than subject now of woe.
All mental pangs, by time's kind laws,
  Hast lost the power to know.

O death! Thou awe-inspiring prince,
  That keepst the world in fear;
Why dost thou tear more blest ones hence,
  And leave him ling'ring here?

The Bear Hunt

A wild-bear chase, didst never see?
  Then hast thou lived in vain.
Thy richest bump of glorious glee,
  Lies desert in thy brain.

When first my father settled here,
  'Twas then the frontier line:
The panther's scream, filled night with fear
  And bears preyed on the swine.

But wo for Bruin's short lived fun,
　　　When rose the squealing cry;
Now man and horse, with dog and gun,
　　　For vengeance, at him fly.

A sound of danger strikes his ear;
　　　He gives the breeze a snuff;
Away he bounds, with little fear,
　　　And seeks the tangled rough.

On press his foes, and reach the ground,
　　　Where's left his half munched meal;
The dogs, in circles, scent around,
　　　And find his fresh made trail.

With instant cry, away they dash,
　　　And men as fast pursue;
O'er logs they leap, through water splash,
　　　And shout the brisk halloo.

Now to elude the eager pack,
　　　Bear shuns the open ground;
Through matted vines, he shapes his track
　　　And runs it, round and round.

The tall fleet cur, with deep-mouthed voice,
　　　Now speeds him, as the wind;
While half-grown pup, and short-legged fice,
　　　Are yelping far behind.

And fresh recruits are dropping in
      To join the merry corps:
With yelp and yell—a mingled din—
      The woods are in a roar.

And round, and round the chase now goes,
      The world's alive with fun;
Nick Carter's horse, his rider throws,
      And more, Hill drops his gun.

Now sorely pressed, bear glances back,
      And lolls his tired tongue;
When as, to force him from his track,
      An ambush on him sprung.

Across the glade he sweeps for flight,
      And fully is in view.
The dogs, new-fired, by the sight,
      Their cry, and speed, renew.

The foremost ones, now reach his rear,
      He turns, they dash away;
And circling now, the wrathful bear,
      They have him full at bay.

At top of speed, the horsemen come,
      All screaming in a row.
"Whoop! Take him Tiger—Seize him Drum"—
      Bang—bang—the rifles go.

And furious now, the dogs he tears,
    And crushes in his ire.
Wheels right and left, and upward rears,
    With eyes of burning fire.

But leaden death is at his heart,
    Vain all the strength he plies,
And, spouting blood from every part,
    He reels, and sinks and dies.

And now a dinsome clamor rose,
    'Bout who should have his skin.
Who first draws blood, each hunter knows,
    This prize must always win.

But who did this, and how to trace
        What's true from what's a lie,
Like lawyers, in a murder case
        They stoutly argufy.

Aforesaid fice, of blustering mood,
        Behind, and quite forgot,
Just now emerging from the wood,
        Arrives upon the spot.

With grinning teeth, and up-turned hair—
        Brim full of spunk and wrath,
He growls, and seizes on dead bear,
        And shakes for life and death.

And swells as if his skin would tear,
    And growls, and shakes again;
And swears, as plain as dog can swear,
    That he has won the skin.

Conceited whelp! We laugh at thee—
    Now mind, that not a few
Of pompous, two-legged dogs there be,
    Conceited quite as you.